# The World that Jack Built

From Trauma to Recovery:
Embracing the Child Within Through Poetry

Copyright © 2024 Honor Hope

Published by Star Light Publishing

Paperback ISBN: 978-1-0686681-0-4
eBook ISBN: 978-1-0686681-1-1

All rights reserved

No part of this book may be reproduced in any form or by any electronic or mechanical means, including in information storage and retrieval systems, without permission in writing from the author, with the exception of short excerpts used in a review.

This book is a work of non-fiction. While the poems draw from real experiences and events, some names and details may have been changed to respect privacy. Any resemblance to persons, living or dead, or actual events is intended to be authentic.

# The World that Jack Built

From Trauma to Recovery:
Embracing the Child Within Through Poetry

Honor Hope

# The World That Jack Built

My name is Honor Hope

This is the first of four books that reflect how your inner child can become separated creating his or her own personality as result of traumatic childhood events.

In the books I explore through the form of poetry how I myself came to recognise my inner child's voice and allowed expression. This is the first book in where I met Jack, my five year old inner child; this is an account of the conversations which took place. Through giving Jack his voice both he and I were able to heal together.

Through making this book public I aim to help other people to understand the concept of inner child, and that recovery is possible. In the future I will be publishing the remaining three books, in which Jack grows up and meets my second inner child Hope, a 16 year old girl.

From being able to identify, communicate and connect with my own inner children I have been able to learn techniques which I call NICE therapy (Nurturing Inner Child Emotions) to allow others to make this connection with their own inner child, in order for them and their inner child to be at peace with one another.

The inner children will only be happy when they have been given the opportunity to grow through expressing themselves to you.

I am the founder of the company Inner Hope; the company offers a myriad of services that enable the clients to heal themselves through a range of mediums. We offer Rahanni Celestial Healing, Crystal Healing, NICE Therapy and Healing through Art. All of these services are individually tailored to the client.

If after reading this book you would like any information or guidance about the book or Inner Hope's services please feel free to contact me via email: suziiddon10@icloud.com or phone: 07399237359.

Much Love and Light

# Contents

| | | |
|---|---|---|
| 1 | Toys in Need | 11 |
| 2 | Him | 13 |
| 3 | Let It Be | 16 |
| 4 | The Monster | 18 |
| 5 | This is the Puppet Master (My Dad) | 20 |
| 6 | Lullaby | 23 |
| 7 | Understanding | 27 |
| 8 | Rebellion | 31 |
| 9 | Chains | 34 |
| 10 | Chain Number One | 39 |
| 11 | Jack is Angry | 42 |
| 12 | What is Going on Jack? | 47 |
| 13 | The Special Christmas Tree | 51 |
| 14 | Jack Makes Snowballs | 57 |
| 15 | Christmas Day | 61 |
| 16 | Wake Up Jack | 66 |
| 17 | The Easter Bunny | 70 |
| 18 | Jack Wants to Remove His Chains | 75 |
| 19 | The Puppet Master | 81 |
| 20 | Nothing Is Enough Jack | 84 |
| 21 | Jack is in a Rage Once More | 87 |
| 22 | The Puppet Master is Dead | 90 |
| 23 | Jack Wants a Dad | 93 |
| 24 | John HEAL – from Jack | 96 |
| 25 | John HEAL – from Me | 100 |

| | | |
|---|---|---|
| 26 | Jack's Revenge | 103 |
| 27 | The Puppet Master Returns | 105 |
| 28 | The Puppet Master's Trick | 107 |
| 29 | Jack's Praise | 111 |
| 30 | Now Has Come the Time | 113 |

# Key Code for Fonts

Jack
Suzi
**Puppet Master**
Jack's Ideal Dad

# Toys in Need

You brought me many gifts
Each time you passed me by
A teddy with one ear
A doll with a missing eye

To others it was tat
Toys no longer required
Probably because they were old and that
New ones had been acquired

But to me they were precious
I did not care that they were old
Each toy had a story
Which never could be told

They could not tell you what happened
Because they could not speak
But I would give them comfort
As it was what these toys did seek

Someone who would love them
For what they were inside
To see past that tattered look
And hold them up with pride

So I would treat them kindly
And brush my dolly's hair
Tell them I would tend them
And treat them with loving care

I would tell them that I understood
How unhappy they had been
But there are some nice people
And not everyone is mean

I would tell them that the dustbin men
Had given me a special deed
That is why they gave me
These special toys in need

I would tell them that the dustbin men
Were very kind to me
As they were the ones that saw
What others did not see

Just like I could see
How special these toys were
And see beyond the surface
Of teddy's matted fur

# 2

# Him

Our eyes were a book
A dead giveaway
Of what we did see
Day after day

The shouting and name calling
Was hard to bear
Then came the slaps
And grabbing of hair

Punches and kicks were a regular event
These were how lots of our days were spent
Watching scenes, blinded by tears
Memories of a lifetime – but only four years

Relaxing a little
When he went out a while
Maybe even managing
A bitter sweet smile

*The World that Jack Built*

Try to pick up the pieces
Stop mum from crying
Forgetting our own tears
That still needed drying

When the tea towel is discarded
We tidy the place
Try not to stare
At her swollen red face

Her pain was ours
And his was his own
Then we'd wait
For him to come home

Air would get tenser
As time ticked by
Breathing was faster
We all knew why

Then he'd arrive
Happy as Larry
He never had any
Guilt to carry

We would breathe united a big sigh of relief
Praying there was nothing bubbling beneath
We would retreat to our beds with a heavy heart
And pray we wouldn't be woken with another start

Sleep and see what a new day would bring
Maybe we'll laugh and maybe we'll sing
Or maybe it will happen all over again
and we will stay in our house of fear and pain

## 3

## Let It Be

Let the tears be dried
By someone's kindly hand
Let someone just whisper
I really understand

Let someone just hold me
Wipe my tears away
To have someone's arms embrace me
Would make it seem ok

Let my heart be given
Some tender loving care
Please let someone notice
My torment and despair

Let someone be sent to listen
An angel from the sky
Who can really comfort me
When needed as I cry

Let someone say don't worry
You are not at all to blame
You can hold your head up now
Don't keep it down in shame

I ask for one last thing
The icing on the cake
Let me be somewhere else
When I finally wake

## 4

## The Monster

Tell me who it is
Tell me who you are
You're making me feel scared right now
And mum and dad are far

It's dark and it's scary
With shadows on the wall
With spooky noises and silhouettes
For kids like us so small

The shadows are like claws
Getting ready to attack
Huddle up the window all
But never turn your back

After what seems an eternity
We make our great escape
Desperate to open windows
Meant to keep us safe

Fighting for survival
Who will be the last
To stay with spooky noises
And a heart that beats so fast

As we all run screaming
Up the street lit path
Suddenly in the distance
We hear a familiar laugh

Dad must be there
He's not even afraid
Let's go back home
And hope it's gone we prayed

We get back to the house
The light would once more glow
"Where is the monster dad?"
We tried to find you so

But you were here
We'd thought you'd gone
**"There is no monster kids
You must have got it wrong**

**I've been here all the time
It must be in your mind"**
So we all go to bed and dream
The dreams of monster kind

# 5

## This is the Puppet Master
## (My Dad)

The Puppet Master is feeling very powerful
He believes he is invincible

I am the one and only
I am the Puppet Master, you see
I pull your strings and use your limbs
To create your misery

I decide if you will be
happier than yesterday
And I'll decide if you will leave your box
So you can have a play

If you leave your box and see the world
I'll make damn sure you're scared
Your perception of people
I'll make sure will be impaired

*This is the Puppet Master (My Dad)*

You will become so very twisted
I'll turn you into me
For I am the Puppet Master
Who will NEVER set you free

Your strings will be a mess
Of knots, to keep you restricted
You'll always be that mess
As the Puppet Master predicted

If I decide to let you
Have a happy face
I will pull your strings again
And show you my disgrace

You have no right to smile
Or feel good about who you are
Because *I'M THE ONLY MASTER*
*I AM THE BEST BY FAR*

You really are a toy to me
To keep me entertained
When I am bored with one
The others still remain

You will never know who you are
Or where you do belong
As the puppet is so weak
And the master, <u>*oh so strong*</u>

I will never tire of my game
The one of mind control
Because while I decide to stay the same
You never will feel whole

You will never dare to leave me
Because you are so weak
So just you sit and wait
To feel my little *tweak*

# 6

## Lullaby

There is something that controls me
It drains my very soul
Never to let me rest
Or allow me to feel whole

It takes over every time
Twisting my childish mind
Lying there in wait
Until I meet someone kind

It will not just let me be
And enjoy my sacred time
It whispers in my ear
And chants it eerie rhyme

*Are you sure they really like you?
You know you get things wrong
Don't believe them, you won't get hurt
If you hear my little song*

*The World that Jack Built*

Listen to me
Cos I'm the one who will never let you down
I'm the one that's with you
When there's no one else around

They'll treat you nice and kindly
And play their part so well
But they are just pretending
I know... I can tell

So I try to carry on
Ignore my trusted friend
Wanting kindness more
Than him who I depend

But then I hear the voice
Much more sinister this time
He whispers in my ear
A slightly different rhyme

"Listen to me carefully
They'll reject you that's for sure
Forget it all, the hugs, the kiss
It will leave you wanting more

Or make the most of it my dear
Drain their very soul
Listen to my voice
It helps you keep control

Drain them of affection
Take whatever you need
Cos you and I are one my dear
We survive on all this greed

You are an emotional vampire
Don't give them the chance to be
Your special friend, your loved one
**Cos I'm your friend you see**

So I fill my void
To the point of overflowing
Feeding hungry minds
To help us both keep growing

Then I toss them to one side
Before they do it to me
And sigh with great relief
Because he is pleased, you see

But now I feel alone
More than I did before
Because he has taken what I had
So now I am wanting more

In the distance I hear his voice
Soon you will hear my rhyme
Cos I am your little lullaby
'Til the end of time

When he comes again
I feel how much he has grown
Because I always feed him
It's all I've ever known

## 7

## Understanding

Come closer my little friend
Because now has come the time
Where you must try to listen
And hear my special rhyme

You have been with me since a child
You have served me very well
You gave me words of comfort
Whilst living in my hell

You gave me so much solace
When things were hard to bear
With the violence and the tension
I needed someone there

I never really understood my friend
Why I became more needy
But now I know the truth
You became more greedy

YOU are the emotional vampire
That drains my very soul
YOU are the one that stops me
From being in control

Because you are the one who is insecure
And craving for affection
And you are the one who cannot face
Or cope with more rejection

But now the child has gone
It is time you merged with me
So we can both move on
And set each other free

Because you are me, and I am you
Until the end of time
So listen carefully my little one
Listen to mummy's rhyme

We were bound only by sadness
And memories of childhood years
The reason we both survived
Is we fed each other's fears

But this is not the end for you
It's the beginning, a fresh new start
Together we can work
On healing both our hearts

**I will tend you now**
You need not fear rejection
Because you are my little one
I will give you much affection

You do not have to guard me now
It is not needed anymore
Because you were guarding the child
And I am the child no more

Your job is done, it is time for me
To sing you lullabies
Where you can sleep and rest a while
And close your weary eyes

Then when you wake, you will see the change
I will be a woman through and through
Then you will feel much clearer
About what you have to do

You can be that inner child
Whose focus on life is fun
You can show me how to do things
Things I've never done

We will roll down hills
And catch fish in nets
We will blow bubbles in the sun
And see how big they get

So what do you say my little one?
Do you accept my little rhyme?
That I will be *your* lullaby
Until the end of time

I'm glad you feel much stronger now
For I was feeling weary
I was fed up being the one
That made your life so dreary

You see I couldn't stop it
Until you set me free
So we can be together
And one identity

I accept I need to rest now
And the guarding part is done
And when you wake me this time
I will teach you how to have fun

I know that you will save me
I no longer have to fear
Cos now my mum is back
And I will always have her near

## 8

## Rebellion

I told you to go to sleep
And rest your weary eyes
Have you forgotten already?
That I am the one so wise

Remember I do not need
Your protection anymore
Listen to what I am saying
I am not the girl anymore

I know it is not easy
For you to go to sleep
Even if you close your eyes
You are always ready to peep

Waiting for it to happen
Protecting my fragile heart
Being so very fatherly
How well you play your part

But you know I am not the child
I am an adult now you see
So rest my little one
Let me, your mother, be

*I know I am making it difficult
I just don't know how to rest
Each time I shut my eyes
I'm reminded of my quest*

*Your one and only protector
Who will remain by your side
So you suffer no more rejection
And hurt no more inside*

*It's easier for you
To put on that false smile
But I see the truth mum
You can only do it a while*

*Don't do what they did
And push my fears away
You said you were my mother
And said that you would stay*

I promise not to reject you
Or push your fears away
I will give you love
Each and everyday

You need not have to worry
I understand your fears
Just as you understood my child
All my childhood tears

But you need to try and sleep
And ease your troubled mind
And try to be *just* happy
When I'm meeting someone kind

If I get rejected
Or start to lose hope
It's not the end of the world
Because you will help me cope

So go to sleep a while now
And hear my little rhyme
Because I'm your little lullaby
Until the end of time

*I will try to sleep now*
*I'll really try my best*
*Cos I am very tired*
*And I know I need the rest.*

# 9

## Chains

You are still not sleeping little one
If you are it is very light
Do not sleep with one eye open
Embrace your rest, don't fight

When you do not sleep
You get so very mad
About the things you want
And the things you never had

You conjure up many images
Of what you want and need
But I am your mum, I know what is best
For both of us to succeed

You have worn yourself right out
You feel so very drained
But then you scream and shout
And you have to be restrained

*Chains*

I know you will find it difficult
To lie and sleep a while
And when you throw your tantrums
It kind of makes me smile

But that man is not my father
Neither is he yours
He is not the one
To open many doors

This man is not my partner
He is someone with whom I dance
You cannot force relationships
You must leave it up to chance

He appeals to you my sweet
As he is a contrast of our dad
He seems so kind and caring
Like the one we never had

*But I want him for your partner
So you can feel his warm embrace
For him to say I love you
And gently cup your face*

But now is not the time
For relationships so deep
Because you are more important
Other ones will keep

When we merge as one
That will be the time
For both of us to sing
A new and happy rhyme

But that is a long way off
We have much work to do
For now it is just the time
For only me and you

So what do you say little one
Tell me how you feel
So I can listen as your mum
And help your heart to heal

*I really get upset
When we get so very near
To finding someone loving
And embracing us so dear*

*Anyone will do
As long as they are kind
Then we can sleep and dream
But not the monster kind*

*Where we will wake with a happy heart
Knowing that he is there
Knowing he will comfort
In our times of despair*

I really want it badly
More than I can express
To be shown that kind of loving
That special tenderness

*I want it now, I really do*
*I know I sound a brat*
*But this is so important*
*Can nobody else see that?*

I want to be so happy
Please help to set me free
Unlock all these chains mum
That take the breath from me

I feel such suffocation
These thoughts inside my head
Weigh heavy on my heart
Like a piece of lead

I feel so very agitated
Kind of wriggly, you know
I want to stretch my arms and legs
I really want to grow

But these chains they do restrict me
They sometimes make me weep
They dig in my tired eyes
When I try to sleep

*How can you help me mum?*
*What are we going to do?*
*How can we be as one?*
*And be whole through and through*

As there are so many chains my sweet
There are many keys to find
This is not an easy task
So it will take some time

But we will work together
And open all the doors
So we can live a happy life
For now and ever more

## 10

## Chain Number One

Your eyes are bound by chains
So you do not have to see
They keep you in the dark
Is that the place to be?

Mum the dark is very scary
But there is a benefit you see
Cos' if I can't see him
Then he can't see me

I can stay safe in my hiding place
And pretend that I'm not here
And then he will not notice
My eyes are full of fear

When he used to see the fear
That made it so much worse
He would go from being nice
To someone who spoke so terse

When I saw his face
I'd get really scared you know
Why did you leave me mum?
When I needed you so

Call yourself a mother
Desert me in my hour
So I am all alone with him
To cringe and to cower

I don't see what you see
When you want to love a man
All I see is fear again
Get out while I can

Leave me be I don't want this
I'm just a little one
"Be a good girl" his voice would hiss
I introduce chain number one

So how can you do them things?
It makes me feel quite ill
And how can you do them things
With your own free will

Cos you are doing things
That caused me so much pain
And I don't want to do it
No more, not ever again

*Chain Number One*

My eyes are very sore
As these chains are very rusty
They are so very old
But keep them I must, you see

So I do not see his eyes
And he cannot see mine
And I will be protected
Until the end of time

Cos if he doesn't see me
He cannot see my fear
And if I don't see him
Was he ever really here?

## II

## Jack is Angry

Why do you not listen
When I tell you about my eyes
You have not spoken since
You've ignored my inner cries

You said that you would help me
To deal with all my pain
But you've rejected me once more
**You've done it once again**

Why do you think I'm lying mum?
I'm not, I told the truth
This is a part of you as well
A burden of your youth

What happened to me, happened to you
You can not reject your past
Even though it's gone now
Memories always last

I have no memory of these events
So I find it hard to feel
And even though it has happened
It does not seem so real

You said that I rejected you
In your hour of despair
I suppose I must accept this
Because I was never there

I must have been somewhere else
My mind another place
And that is why I forgot
His hair, his eyes, his face

I do not disbelieve you
But you need to help me feel
What you felt back then
So I can help you heal

I didn't mean to reject you
I thought I'd disappear
I was trying to protect you
In your childish year

The idea was to fade away
And take you somewhere safe
But you must have stayed behind
That is why you saw his face

It is a terrible thing to happen
You must have been so scared
It must have been even worse
To think I never cared

To think I left you all alone
To face that scary man
And deal with all your fear and pain
The best way that you can

But when I went away like that
To my friendly place
I thought you were right behind me
Not looking at his face

Because I could never look back
And see those scary eyes
Because if he saw the fear
He would win the prize

But he still saw you
Your eyes so full of terror
I have to admit my huge mistake
And sorry for my judgement error

Why did you not come with me?
Why did you stay behind?
*Because you went so quick*
*Your place I could not find*

*Jack is Angry*

I went to the beach you know
Awash with sea and sand
And while I walked along the shore
I went to take your hand

But you were not there
I could not swap my place
To somewhere I could see
His really scary face

So I chose to stay
And you suffered every time
And I was truly guilty
Of this awful crime

Abandonment of my child
All because of fear
Never really telling him
Things that he should hear

Letting him believe
He deserves to be left behind
For fear of returning
For my little one to find

It's not your fault, it never was
I'm sorry I was never there
I'm sorry that you suffered
And thought I didn't care

You are my child, and I love you dear
You are a part of me
We will work together
To set each other free

I'm feeling so much better
Because we've talked like this
It's really just as healing
As a hug or kiss

Cos now I know you were scared
As much as I was too
It's helped me understand
Mum I forgive you.

## 12

## What is Going on Jack?

Tell me what is happening Jack
You are hurting us again
I really cannot take anymore
Of all this extra pain

Why do you feel so angry?
I feel your burning wrath
The volcano has erupted
But we still have aftermath

Devastation is all around
Swirling around my mind
Negative angry thoughts
Like those of a previous kind

I really want to help you
But you are making me real low
These major changes you have had
I thought would help you grow

We need to do more work
And get through this together
We are bound for life
Emotions last forever

Remember if you hurt
Then also, so do I
Just like any mother does
When her son does cry

I am willing to listen
I am here for you, you know
Let us not meet someone kind
And tell him just to go

Why are you so tense
With someone who is so nice
See me as your counsel
Who will give you good advice

I am really sorry mum
I feel so very down
My smile that has disappeared
Is replaced with a frown

It was nice whilst it lasted
But now I feel so mad
It is slipping away so quickly
The relationship we had

You have no time for me anymore
Now that you have got him
The one that cares so much
Filling you to the brim

You have turned greedy mum
You have kept him to yourself
You never shared his warmth
You left me on the shelf

What happened to all the promises
Of showing me so much fun
Its Christmas time you know
And there is nothing that we've done

Nothing at all
Where is the Christmas Tree
Where is all the sparkle
That every child should see

You got so carried away
By a bastard of a man
Keep up the good work mum
Do more damage while you can

Twist the knife a little more
Push it deep inside
Because I feel so worthless now
I want to sit and hide

*The World that Jack Built*

*That is how I feel*
*So what you gonna do*
*You said you were going to help me to heal*
*Just me and you*

I really am so sorry
That you feel like this
I will give you a warm embrace
On your cheek I will plant a kiss

Please forgive me son
For being rather slack
For getting carried away
Seeming to turn my back

Tomorrow we will hang decorations
Of sparkly things that are nice
We will talk about Santa
And his sleigh that rides on ice

So go to sleep for now
Have dreams of things that glisten
When you wake we will be ready to talk
And we will both be ready to listen

## 13

## The Special Christmas Tree

Its Christmas little one
It's time to do the tree
With all things sparkly, like tinsel
For little ones to see

What do you want to do first?
Where do you wish to start?
Oh I'm so excited mum
I've got a happy heart

He looks at the tree then says...
The lights must go on first
Squealing with excitement
I think he's going to burst

Okay Jack, wind them round the tree
And I will feed them through
This is a very big job
For a little boy like you

*I promise I'll do it good mum*
*It will really look the best*
I know it will, you are a clever boy
I am sure I will be impressed

That is the way, you have made it grand
Now I will plug them in
So you can see them twinkle
And I can see your grin

I plug them in and stare
At the wonder on Jack's face
With the rosiest little cheeks
Perfect features set in place

The smile that emerges
Lightens my mood some more
Something that I have never seen
In his eyes before

*What's next mum?*
*What shall we do?*
*Can we hang on baubles?*
*Which are shiny and new*

After switching off the lights
I pass Jack the balls
Little fingers clutching tight
So they do not fall

He asks me for a colour
Because that is his favourite hint
In between blue and green
Like the colour of mint

After hanging on the balls
His face is glowing now
But then it slightly changes
He has a furrowed brow

What is the matter Jack?
Why do you look so worried?
I'm thinking mum does it look no good?
Cos I done it rather hurried

It looks beautiful my dear
Perfect in every way
You would not find one better
In a window shop display

He puffs out his chest
And steps back to admire his work
He stops a minute for a rest
With a look that holds a smirk

I want to put the tinsel on
With colours of every sort
It really will sparkle mum
Like you my child, I thought

So he puts on every colour
Purple, red and blue
The silvers and the golds
And many other hue

I tell him it looks pretty
Now he must close his eyes real tight
Only to open them again
When I switch out the big light

He looks at me with annoyance
*You can't switch out the light mum*
*Cos we won't be able to see*
*All the pretty things*
*That are hanging on the tree*

I give a little chuckle
And stroke his curly hair
Now I see the reason
For his look of despair

Sweetheart it is better
To switch the big light out
For the colours will be brighter
Trust me Jack, don't pout

I switch off the light
And cover his eyes
Switching on the fairy lights
For little Jack's surprise

When I let him see
The tree in all its splendour
The picture on his face
Is one I shall remember

*Oh mum! It looks so pretty*
*But not as pretty as you*
*You are prettier than anything*
*I really do love you*

I give him a loving hug
And tell him I love him too
But there is one more thing little Jack
It is the most important thing to do

*What is it mum?*
*Tell me what it is*
It is the angel little one
Something we must not miss

I will lift you up
And you must place her carefully on the tree
Right on the very top
So she looks after you, you see

Because she will look down
And keep you safe in her wings
Wrapping you up in silk
And all your treasured things

So he puts her on the tree
With a very happy yawn
He wore himself right out
With the tree he did adorn

He names it Angel Day

## 14

## Jack Makes Snowballs

*Look outside mum*
*The ground it is all white*
*It wasn't like that*
*When I went to bed last night*

It has been snowing little man
The first time you have seen
The ground that looks like sugar
With a light coating of cream

*Ooh that sounds nice*
*Can I eat it? Try a little taste?*
*If I promise to eat it all...*
*Leaving none to waste*

You cannot eat it little man
It does not taste so nice
It is frozen water
That turns to snow and ice

*Ugh I don't like it now*
*Water tastes real bad*
But the snow is fun to play in Jack
As long as you are well clad

After breakfast I will show you how
To make snowballs, snowmen too
We will get a carrot for his nose
And make him just like you

For now you go and see
This list of things to find
Buttons, scarf and a hat
Sticks of any kind

He dashes off with excitement
*Look mum, I've found them all*
Well done, you are a clever boy
Do not run, you will fall

Jack is wrapped up warm
Little nose glowing red
I tell him he is like Rudolph
*"Yes the flying Reindeer" he said*

First we make the snowballs
Bigger and bigger each time
Look Jack, yours is huge!
It is much bigger than mine

He looked happy for a minute
Then he looked quite sad
*I am going to help you mum*
*Make the biggest one you've had*

Oh you are so thoughtful Jack
You are very kind to me
If we roll it up together
It will be the best you see

So we unite all our forces
We are big and strong
Helping one another
To push the ball along

Our ball became that big
A snowman's body is made
We are so excited
For our work to be displayed

Then we make the head
Jack fills in his face
We name him Little Jack Frost
This is his special place

Jack wraps a scarf
Around the snowman's neck
Kissing him on the cheek
That tiny childish peck

*Mum where's his hat?*
I will get it son
He places it on his head
Finally a job well done

Look at Jack, little man
He is smiling, do you see?
*That's because he's happy*
*It's because he's me*

I take Jack indoors
Make chocolate to warm him through
You have made the best snowman Jack
I am very proud of you

He curls up in a ball
Head tucked in my side
That happy contented smile
Which makes me warm inside

I do not need hot chocolate,
Soup or a cup of tea
For Jack warms me through and through
When he smiles at me

## 15

## Christmas Day

Wake up little man
For it is Christmas Day you see
There are many delights
Under your special Christmas Tree

Because Santa Claus has been
He has left many toys
For all the little people
For special girls and boys

So on his early start
He gives the sweetest grin
Rubbing his eyes with little fists
He asks... *How did he get in?*

He came down the chimney
When the children were asleep
He has so many promises
For little ones to keep

Because Santa is a man
Who hears your every word
If you want something badly
Your voice, it will be heard

He asks his little elves
To help him make the toys
So he can deliver them Christmas Eve
To the special girls and boys

As we walk into the lounge
Jack has a big surprise
The ceiling is full of decorations
His joy he can't disguise

*Wow it looks so pretty mum*
*What shall we do now?*
It is time to see your presents Jack
I give a little bow

First go see your stocking
With the red and white trim
Have a look inside
To see what lies within

He unwraps little gifts
Of chocolate coins and things
Stopping for a moment
To look at angel wings

Just like a reflection
Of one to the other
He has the face of an angel
I am proud to be his mother

He squeals with excitement
As he pulls out a big blue truck
*Look at this one mum*
*I can fill the back with muck*

You are a clever boy I say
As I sit and cup his cheeks
Kissing him on the nose
Seeing changes over weeks

After the stocking's done
We go and call his dad
He is a truly lovely man
Not like the one we had

His dad picks him up
*Hello soldier, what have you got? Let's see*
*I've got a big blue truck dad*
*Will you sit and play with me?*

He doesn't need to be asked twice
He plays for quite some time
I come in from the kitchen
And call "it is breakfast time"

We sit and we talk in the kitchen
As we dine
I feel so very blessed
With this precious family of mine

Then we go to the tree
All full of tints and hues
The little one's favourites
Are the greens and the blues

From the unwrapping of the presents
And stories from his dad
Of all the things that are magic
And none of which are bad

Jacks little face is glowing
Of happiness and love
Looking at the angel
On the tree above

My baby looks so sleepy
It has been a tiring day
Come on little man
It's bed for you I say

As I tuck him in
And say goodnight my dear
His dad walks in behind me
And gently tickles his ear

Goodnight soldier,
You're my favourite little man
We will keep you safe
And make you happy as we can

Because you are our special one
The very, very best
Shut your eyes my precious son
It is time for you to rest

## 16

## Wake Up Jack

Wake up Jack, my precious little one
And open your sleepy eyes
There is a special job to be done
For one so very wise

Our lovely Christmas tree
Needs to have a rest
So when she comes out next year
She will surely look her best

Jack gives me a little scowl
What is the matter little man
Give your mum a smile
I know that you can

*I don't want to take it down
I like my special tree
We made it really nice
Together you and me*

We need to take it down Jack
As she is feeling tired you know
When she has a rest
It will help the tree to grow

*Oh I see, Okay mum*
*We'll take it down today*
*Like we did before*
*In a very special way*

We take the decorations off
Jack is giggling like mad
Looking at his reflection
And a new face that he had

Unwinding shiny tinsel
With tiny fingers small
Looking up at his tree
His stretches his arms out tall

*I want to be a tree mum*
*A special one like this*
Trees must grow my precious son
I will plant you with a kiss

Do you want to grow Jack?
Or stay like this some more?
*I like the size I am for now*
*It makes me feel secure*

Then stay as you are my sweet
Until you are ready to be a tree
Then you will grow in every way
Maybe bigger than me!

He stands and stares a while
With his hands he cups my face
*I want a cuddle mum*
I respond with a warm embrace

*Can I keep you he says*
*Will you always be my mum?*
Yes I will my sweet
Because you will always be my son

The angel comes off last
Looking oh so small
Against the tree so vast
Magnificent and tall

We put the tree away
Jack is quiet once again
*The room looks so empty mum*
*It makes me feel the same*

So I tell Jack if he wants
He can keep the angel on the shelf
His face turns from frown to grin
Like a cheeky little elf

My little boy asks to be lifted
So he can put his angel away
Beautiful and gifted
He names this Angel Day

## 17

## The Easter Bunny

Wake up little one
You are in for a big surprise
The Easter Bunny is here
You will not believe your eyes

Come and have some breakfast
Then in the garden we will run
To find the eggs the bunny left
And have much Easter fun

Jack rubs his weary eyes
With little fists clenched tight
He has a worried look
One that seems like fright

What is the matter sweet?
Do you not want to see
The colourful trail of eggs
The bunny has left for you and me

*I do mum*
*I want to find them all*
*But the bunny*
*It does frighten me*
*Because it is so tall*

Not everything is scary
If it is so tall
It is just the bad things that happened
You seem to only recall

Tall can be nice
Like the dustbin men, you see?
Remember they were tall
But kind to you and me

And remember how the Christmas tree
Was so big and tall
With all its lights and tinsel
Stood proud against the wall

*Oh yes! I remember those*
*They were very nice*
Good boy Jack, for remembering well
And listening to my advice

Now come let us eat
So we can have some fun
We'll have a hearty breakfast
Followed by a hot-cross bun

We share our Easter breakfast
Paint eggs in different hue
Jack lifts up a green one
*"Look mum this is just for you"*

Good boy Jack
I will put it in a special place
It will be treasured very much
Like you, as I stroke his face

We go out to the garden
With all the bulbs in flower
He's searching here and there
For chocolate to devour

His dad jumps out on him
Jack is squealing with delight
See my little one
Even good dads cause a fright

Dad chases him round the garden
While I don my new disguise
Look out Jack
Be prepared, you are in for a big surprise

As dad stops the chase
And takes him by the hand
They are searching for the eggs
In their Easter Bunny Land

*The Easter Bunny*

Jack finds blue ones, pink ones
Ones with hints of red
And there I sit in hiding
With Bunny ears on my head

Dad keeps up with the game
Did you hear that Jack?
Yes he whispers, what is it?
It is the Bunny, he has come back

If you are real quiet,
he might just let you see
Where he has left some eggs,
By ribbons on a tree

Jack is real quiet
And coming close real fast
I am trying to stifle a giggle
Finding it difficult to last

So I seize my opportunity
And show my great disguise
With my long tall ears and fluffy tail
Jack can't believe his eyes

I have got a Bunny mask on
With whiskers and a velvet nose
He seems somewhat shocked at first
Then his grin, it grows

*It is you mum, it's you!*
*I thought it was*
*The Easter Bunny*
*With ears poking through*

I chase him in a circle
Pretending to hop and skip
But this daft Easter Bunny
On a stone does trip

We fall on the floor with laughter
Tears rolling down our cheeks
See little Jack what happened
Even Bunnies like hide and seek

*That was real good fun mum*
*And I found eggs for me to eat*
*The Easter bunny was kind*
*To leave us such a treat*

Not all tall people are scary
Like I thought they were before
Good boy Jack I am glad it helped
To make you more secure

## 18

## Jack Wants to Remove His Chains

I'm feeling so much better now
I've had this time to rest
I didn't know it at the time
But it was really for the best

Things seem so much clearer now
I can see a chink of light
After living in the dark so long
It really seems quite bright

I feel it's come the time
For these rusty chains to go
They really do restrict me
And I want the chance to grow

They no longer need to protect me
Because I have my mother
Once they have gone, they've gone
I do not want another

The chains have been a part of me
For far too many years
Rubbing skin and scratching me
Rusted by my tears

I want to lose these chains
I want to find the key
For the first time in my life
I want to be set free

Can we start this now mum?
Let's do it here and now
But wait, I do want this
But I really don't know how

Do not worry little one
I am with you all the way
Together we will make a game
A game, we both can play

First lets open chain number one
The one around your eyes
You really should let people see
A child so very wise

I have the key right here Jack
Just trust in what I say
I am by your side my sweet
I will never go away

You no longer need to fear
Of what your eyes may see
Trust me little one
It is safe to set you free

*Please be careful mum
I'm feeling very scared
What happens if I cannot see?
Or my visions' been impaired*

You can see a chink of light
So there is nothing wrong you see
*Okay mum, let's do it now
And do it carefully*

The lock opens up
Jack panics once again
Do not worry mummy's here
Let us unwind this rusty chain

As Jack sees more light
He has to squint his eyes
Then he starts to open them
To look at pale blue skies

He shouts at the top of his voice
*"Everybody look at me
It's me, its Jack
Everybody **I CAN SEE**"*

This makes him more excited
To unravel chains much quicker
It doesn't matter anymore
If they are thinner, or much thicker

Then we remove the chains
That surrounded his little ears
The chain that blocked cruel jibes
In his early years

The chain around his heart
Did not need a key
Because it fell apart
It was old and worn you see

The chain around his chest
That held his breath in tight
In case there was more shouting
Or fear of another fight

Then the chain around his throat
For fear of speaking his mind
For fear of hurting feelings
Only wanting to be kind

No chains around your neck now
So you can hold your head up high
Never to be ashamed again
Just because you cry

*Jack Wants To Remove His Chains*

No chains around you arms now
So you really can embrace
Without fear or humiliation
Or made to feel shamefaced


No chains around your hands now
No fear of how they are used
You are such a kind boy
You never could abuse


No chains around your legs Jack
To stop you moving on
You are finally free son
Your chains they have all gone


How does it feel to be yourself ?
Not foetal anymore
Having freedom to stretch and kick
Restricted by chains no more


But Jack, he is not listening
He is too busy having fun
Enjoying new found freedom
Playing in the sun


I give him a loving cuddle
Then decide to give him space
But as I pull away
I see tears stream down his face

I panic and I think for him
Has it all been far too much?
But then I'm reassured
By his little childish touch

He cups his hands around my face
And tell me they're tears of joy
And he is just so happy now
To be a little boy

I walk a little distance
Because I never leave him, you see
But I want to give him space
To allow him just to be

So as I watch him playing
I revel in his joy
And I feel a mother's love
For my special little boy

## 19

## The Puppet Master

The Puppet Master is back
Playing with his toys
He has so many to play with
It is something he enjoys

He will pull a string to make you smile
Pull another for a frown
If he lifts you up
He will quickly put you down

He sometimes plays more than one
So he can make them fight
Standing them face to face
Laughing at this sight

He makes them lose identity
And takes away their mind
So they really are a toy
A toy, of wooden kind

Because toys they do not feel
They are completely numb inside
They do not even bother now
To try to run and hide

They just accept their fate
Of what is meant to be
But they are bound by him
With strings that no one sees

The toys do not see their strings
Yet they feel that little ***tweak***
The Puppet Masters calling...
Which one does he seek?

When he opens up the toy box
He smells a sense of fear
The puppets in the box
Now cling to enemies dear

The ones they had to fight with
Seem much more friendly now
The Puppet Master's back
Everybody take a bow

He survives on all this glory
Wanting praise for his work
When the day is finally over
He sits back with an eerie smirk

*The Puppet Master*

His toys are lifeless once more
They are emotionally dead
But their strings are still in place
By their arms, their legs, their head

Finally he reaps his reward
His show's a great success
But the puppets in his care
Are left a tangled mess

Their strings are very frazzled
Each time there is less resistance
So he has more control
Over his puppets' sad existence

## 20

## Nothing Is Enough Jack

Jack, what do you think you are doing?
You are making things real tough
The relationship with Paul...
Nothing is enough

No matter what he says
Or does for us, you know
He may as well not bother
Because you cannot let it go

You think they are all the same
Tar them with one brush
Do you not care
My emotions you try to crush

Are you going to punish me
For leaving you back then
For the rest of my life
Over and over again

You must let me help you
To lay this part to rest
You make me feel on edge
By putting him to the test

Because if he makes a mistake
You punish him for a long time
To make him really suffer
For the most terrible of crimes

For being just human
Not perfect in every way
This does not mean he is bad
He just does not know what to say

To be human is very hard
As we deal with people's souls
Trying to fill our own lives
And many other roles

So little Jack
Let us sort it out today
Try to forget previous men
Keep that pain away

Of nasty and cruel words
That penetrate our heart
Sowing seeds of doubt
Let us make a brand new start

I will help you Jack
You need to help me too
Let us blow away the cobwebs
Let the sun shine through

*Okay mum, I'll give it a go*
Jack it will be hard
Really difficult you know
For your past to discard

But when you're feeling angry
Just whisper in my ear
And tell me how you feel
Rather than ranting in fear

*Then you can respond*
*Put my mind at rest*
*Cos you are my mum*
*And you know what's best*

*I am going to sleep a while*
*On waking I'll be refreshed*
*Hopefully by then*
*You'll be feeling much less stressed*

You are a good boy Jack
Very wise I see
When you awaken this time
We will become three

## 21

## Jack is in a Rage Once More

Hello my baby boy
I feel you are angry now
Lashing out, venting rage
Just looking for a row

What gets to you the most
What really gets you mad
What makes your temper flare like this
Turning good to bad

It's him he winds me up
I really feel irate
I want to seek revenge
And decide his terrible fate

He still has control
Over what he makes you think
Thoughts that you are nothing
So you hide away and shrink

Why do you let him do it?
Why are you so weak?
The Puppet Master is back
I felt that little tweak

You said that he was dead
On him you shut the door
But it really is no different
To what it was before

You let him take you over
You become someone new
Someone that is horrid
Someone not like you

When you get so angry
Insecure I feel
I really wanted
To help us both to heal

So why do you get so mad
Cos then it affects me
What you feel, so do I
It's a problem, can't you see?

So when you get annoyed
I get mad, as mad can be
And when you are upset
It breaks my heart you see

*So you need to just reflect*
*On things you say and do*
*Cos they have an effect on me*
*More than they do you*

I hear what you are saying
But never knew it though
I really thought I had learnt
To not let my feelings show

I will try much harder
To be calm, will you do the same?
We were really doing well
To spoil it would be a shame

*Well I will try to sleep now*
*As I am feeling kind of tired*
*Before you wake me up again*
*Could your mood be more retired?*

I will wake you when I am better
Just try to sleep a while
Then I will write you a letter
To say I have a smile

I am glad we talked little one
I understand you more
I will find the Puppet Master while you sleep
On us he will close the door

## 22

## *The Puppet Master is Dead*

I am going to call an end
To the Puppet Master's shows
He has finally retired
From the only thing he knows

To be the great performer
Playing with his toys
He has finally gone for good
**Show's over girls and boys**

There will be no more viewing
Starting from today
Of how he torments his puppets
For his sense of play

There will be no more strings
Attached to my wooden face
No feelings of insignificance
Or ones of much disgrace

First of all I **cut** the strings
Being anchored by the hands
These have become so weak now
They **snap** like rubber bands

Then I **burn** the strings
Anchored by the feet
Years of such misuse
Just melt away with heat

Then I **slash** the strings
Anchored by my head
On that final deed
The Puppet Master's **DEAD**.

My head is in a spin
I drop down to the floor
But I cannot allow myself
To be the puppet anymore

So with my aching limbs
And my head still in a whirl
I pull out remaining strings
The real me can unfurl

Life comes to my eyes
My frown becomes a grin
Because I am no longer wooden
No longer owned by ***him***

As I stand up
On my own
I feel a different feeling
One I've hardly known

A feeling where I can stand
And hold my head up high
One where I do not fear
To look him in the eye

The strings that used to bind us
To keep our spirits tethered
Are finally gone for good
**Cut, burnt** and **perfectly severed**

As the Puppet Master leaves
On him, I shut the door
I face the stage and take a bow
And receive a great encore

The people watching this show
Are very happy now
The Puppet Master's gone I shout
As I leave them with a vow

Never will I be ruled
By anyone again
Insignificance is over
Only love will reign

## 23

## Jack Wants a Dad

Fuck you mum
What do you think you're at?
Having feelings for someone, anyone
Especially ones like that

You make me sick
Where do I come in
When all of your thoughts
Are focused just on him

Let's push him aside
Same old story for Jack
Meet a fuckin' man
Stab him in the back

Cos we know I'm worth nothing mother!
A mere voice inside your ear
Nothing but a sponge
Soaking every tear

# The World that Jack Built

I really thought you'd share
Good as well as bad
Are you not aware
If you are happy, I am mad

Cos you keep him all for you
You are a selfish cow
I am part of your past, your future
Most important, I am now

I want a dad for God's sake
He is mine, not yours
Simple as that it is
Stuff the whys and the wherefores

I'm gonna take him away
So he'll never return
All that will be left is the scars
From this hell that you burn

You are scum of the earth
I'll never let you forget
How little you are worth
As long as you let me fret

Remember we are two in one
But I just want the dad
Listen to my voice
Then it won't go bad

Share him half and half
Make him hold you like a father
So I can get my fix
And stop making it harder

Tell him how it is mum
How I want a dad
I really want a good one
Like the one I never had

I'm gonna rest a while now
I am feeling so worn out
When I wake I want it sorted
Let there be no doubt

If you fail this simple task
There will be hell to pay
It isn't much to ask
Or do you want me in the way?

## 24

## John HEAL – from Jack

It's happening again mum
I really feel rejected
How did we not see it coming
It was so undetected

The fact that he is leaving us
Like the others so many times before
Another one deceiving us
These things we can't ignore

It must be us, we are no good
People want to go
What are we doing to put them off?
We really need to know

My little boy, how sad it is
His leaving is quite grim
But it is not a reflection on us
Nor is it on him

*John NEAL from Jack*

People need to live
Their own lives as we know
We cannot keep them forever
They need the chance to grow


It is suffocating remember
When chains crushed you tight
Where you felt so weak
And you had no strength to fight


*I remember mum
It really really hurt, tearing me apart
Finding it hard to breathe
As it bound around my heart*


Good boy Jack
You remember that pain
It is not very nice to relive it
Or remember it again


But it will help you understand
That he needs to move on
And that he will not forget us
Even when he has gone


But if we wrap him in chains
His heart will start to struggle
Let us bless the time that remains
Replace anger with a cuddle

*The World that Jack Built*

Let us kiss him gently
On his loving face
Let him leave our heart
With humility and grace

He is not rejecting us
It is time for him to grow
Maybe teaching others
All the things he knows

So he can help more people
Special ones like you
Breaking away their chains
That are cutting through

*I see now what you mean
Now I understand
Instead of snatching it away
I'll gently slip his hand*

*I'll say goodbye
You've been so kind
Of stories that you've told
To ease my troubled mind*

I am very pleased Jack
That you have come to such a choice
You are a brave little boy
I hear it in your voice

John NEAL from Jack

Go to sleep little man
Know he is not rejecting us
But purely embracing life
Without affecting us

Only in a positive way
With memories left behind
So they can be recaptured
When them we choose to find

## 25

## John HEAL – from Me

When I first met you
Some months ago today
Never could I imagine
That I would feel this way

Shattered is the word
That I am losing someone dear
Praying that in my heart
I can keep you near

Like listening to the breeze
Hearing your soothing voice
Filling my mind with ease
Reminding me I have choice

Gazing at the sun
Feeling your spirit beside
It is OK to have fun
Too many tears you have cried

I am going to grieve for you now
While you are still around

So when you come to leave
My strength will astound

You will be very proud of me
And what I have achieved
Mourning another loss
Yet feeling less bereaved

I am going to remember all the things
That you said to me
Even in a temper
I will work constructively

I pray that once you have left
I will see you again one day
For by that special time
I will have a lot to say

But if I never see you again
The impact you have had on me
With your wisdom and your knowledge
Has helped to set me free

I bless the day I met you
You gave me identity
The real person has come through
For you have helped me find the key

You are a real man

With your tears and sensitive soul
There is no one better than you
For such an important role

But I will give them a chance
And be less childlike
No toy throwing from the pram
Just three simple words "On Your Bike"

# 26

## Jack's Revenge

Mother you reject me
You are a nasty bitch
Have you forgotten mother dear
About our feet that itch?

When your feet do settle
And you feel safe in times of rest
I will always remind you
That you are second best

You are not allowed to feel
The things that other people feel
You are not even allowed
To know of what is real

So you killed the Puppet Master
And said you did it for me
When you snapped the strings that bound you
Part of him became me

I can teach you now
To be alone and empty inside
Just as he did
The day before he died

He taught me well
What right have you to be
That person with much happiness
After what you did to me

You are my puppet now
I will tangle you in knots
You are at my mercy
Never will it stop

Let the battle commence
If you think that you are brave
I am excited by the suspense
And for the power that I crave

I will leave you with one last thought
Before I go to sleep
You will never be free
Your mind is mine to keep

Give up now for I am strong
You thought the Puppet Master was dead
But Mother
You surely got it wrong

## 27

## The Puppet Master Returns

Mum what are you doing?
He don't give a shit about you
What that you believed
Is all ringing true

To him you are nothing
Something to be abused
Insignificant you are
There to be misused

Remember you're not allowed
To be in a happy place
Are the words of the Master
No smile upon your face

He don't give a shit
When you feel upset
He doesn't even phone
That's as good as it gets

Push him away mum
He's screwing with your head
Think about this one...
Is the Puppet Master really dead?

Or were there two all along?
One is dead
One alive
That hates to see his mother thrive

You need me
You always will
Don't think you're safe
just cos I'm still

I will sing you lullabies once more
And keep this cycle of pain
Being good is such a bore
There is nothing for me to gain

So come and get me mother
Feel my little tweak
It really isn't much fun
To have a mother for a freak

## 28

## The Puppet Master's Trick

So you think you've kicked me down
And knocked me to the floor
Well I told you, you were dead
And can pull my strings no more

I thought I'd slashed them all
How wrong I must have been
I must have missed out something
Something I could not have seen

So on my deep reflection
I will search for hidden strings
That twist away in my mind
By all your nasty things

So I take my special light
There are strings the eyes can't see
Not even mine this time
Though they belong to me

*The World that Jack Built*

You do not scare me anymore
Yet you still upset my life
Creating more self-doubt
To my role as mother and wife

My light has now switched on
As I recoil in shock
Because there are fibres to my heart
Though thin, are made of rock

You stand there oh so proud
Of what you do achieve
Because all your evil thoughts
I am forced to receive

Because of all these thoughts
Can only filter through
You give bad to me
But I give kind to you

I am almost sympathetic
To your very lonely life
Until the light shines brighter
The image cuts like a knife

It does not stop at me
It goes right through to Jack
My god I should have seen it
You are setting him right back

Inner strength surges right through me
As I protect my precious son
With my power of visualisation
I call my spirit one

In seconds she is beside me
Gentle smile on her face
The Puppet Master starts to fight
But she puts him in his place

He cannot even move now
He is frozen to the spot
As she pours love at the fibres
My heart becomes quite hot

In a comfortable and happy way
I stand a bit bemused
She's burning fibres of rock
No more can they be used

Then her angel's wings enfold us
And we feel her powerful love
We fit perfectly inside her
Like a hand that fits a glove

I open up my eyes
And look to the ground
The place where he stands
Has shattered rock all around

There is a bright white circle
Around me and little Jack
She has left the badness for the Puppet Master
So he can have it back

I thank my angel dearly
For helping set us free
She glides across the stage
And smiles so tenderly

The Puppet Master leaves now
On us he shuts the door
A depleted man so haggard
Like I have never seen before

I give little Jack a hug
And tell him he was brave
He can rest so easy now
The Puppet Master is in his grave

## Jack's Praise

What a journey you have had my son
You have been a little star
The many feats you have overcome
Just shows you have come so far

Dealing with rejection
And the heartache that it brings
The craving for affection
And people saying nice things

You have worked through your obsessions
Of meeting people new
Learning many lessons
Techniques, to help you through

You have limited your tantrums
When things did not go right
You are my little soldier
Who learned to stand and fight

You have learned that it is normal
For people to be kind
Many relationships in our life
Were not the normal kind

You helped me very much
With the Puppet Masters defeat
When I turned to face the audience
There you sat front seat

The Puppet Masters death
Was mainly down to **you**
I could not let it happen again
What he put you through

You were my inspiration
The focus of victory
I wanted to help my son
The way that he helped me

I am so very proud of you
And all that you achieve
You have shown such courage
In you I do believe

So just remember this
You are my special son
I will never turn my back again
I will always be your mum

## 30

## Now Has Come The Time

Now has come the time
To stop seeking the approval of many
And now I do not care
If I get approval from any

It does not matter anymore
If others disagree
Because I am the one who lives my life
No one else, just me

The ones that seek approval
Are ones with no self esteem
But situations are not black or white
There is always an in between

So even if someone approves
It is irrelevant, you see
Because any mistakes I make
Time will tell, we'll see

Where I will reprimand myself
And learn by what I have done
Whether it's in relation to myself, my daughter
Or my son

I am the biggest judge
To see the error of my ways
Because many judgements are clouded
By searching for that praise

Situations have arisen
Many times in past and present
Where I have known just what to do
But still remain so hesitant

Seeking some approval
Or clarity of doing right
Feeling confused and anxious
Should I, Will I, I might

But now has come the time
To really stand my ground
Whether I am alone
Or others are around

I will make a firm decision
Stick with it all the way
And if I get it wrong
Tomorrow's another day

But if I get it right
I will give myself much praise
And go on looking forward
To new and improved ways

www.ingramcontent.com/pod-product-compliance
Lightning Source LLC
Chambersburg PA
CBHW030451010526
44118CB00011B/890